Made in the USA
Las Vegas, NV
08 May 2024

89681386R00090